Q: WHO HAS THE ANSWER?

No need to raise your hand. This journey of questions is made just for you. Every day for the next three years, you'll have a question along with a prayer or Bible verse to explore. Along the way, you'll discover more about yourself and God's love for you.

There's only one rule—every answer is correct! That's right. So let the surprising, interesting conversation begin. You'll be so glad you asked, "What's the question of the day?"

IDEAS TO STRETCH THE FUN

PARENTS Read the question with your son or daughter. As one of you writes down the answer, let the response and the conversation unfold naturally.

KIDS Do the questions with your family and then write down some of your favorite ones to ask friends whenever you're wondering, "What is there to do around here?"

At the end of the three years, you'll have a keepsake time capsule of ideas, opinions, hopes, happenings, and prayers.

A: YOU HAVE THE ANSWER!

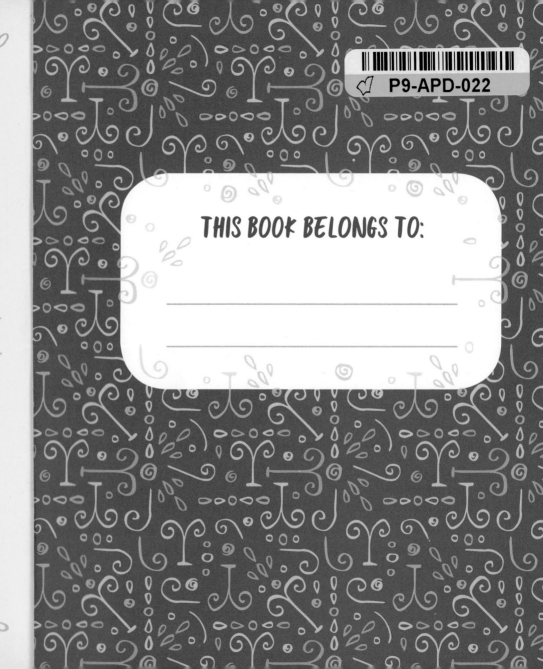

P9-APD-022

THIS BOOK BELONGS TO:

_____

_____

QUESTIO
of th
DAY

HARVEST HOUSE PUBLISHERS
EUGENE, OREGON

JANUARY 1

What do you love about starting something new?

20__ _____

_____

_____

_____

_____

20__ _____

_____

_____

_____

_____

20__ _____

_____

_____

_____

_____

"See, I am doing a new thing! Now it springs up;
do you not perceive it?"—ISAIAH 43:19

How do you feel about answering questions?

20__ _____

_____

_____

_____

20__ _____

_____

_____

_____

20__ _____

_____

_____

_____

_____

Jesus, I am excited to discover more
about who You created me to be.

What do you have fun doing?

20___ _____

_____

_____

_____

20___ _____

_____

_____

_____

20___ _____

_____

_____

_____

God, show me how to delight in life. When I am bored,
remind me of the simple ways I can have fun.

If you were put in charge of $1 million to
give away, how would you do that?

20___ ___

20___ ___

20___ ___

"God loves a cheerful giver." —2 CORINTHIANS 9:7

What is something you believe about God?

20_ _ _____

_____

_____

_____

20_ _ _____

_____

_____

_____

20_ _ _____

_____

_____

_____

_____

*Lord, thank You for loving me. You are big and amazing. I look
forward to learning more about You every year of my life.*

JANUARY 6

If you could only eat two foods for a
month, what would you choose?

20___

20___

20___

God, I am grateful for all the food You provide. I pray today
for people who are in need of food and other basic needs.

JANUARY 7

What is one habit you want to stop?
What is one you'd like to start?

20___ ___

_____

_____

_____

_____

20___ ___

_____

_____

_____

_____

20___ ___

_____

_____

_____

_____

_____

_Jesus, show me how to live in strong and good
ways. Shape my behavior so I can honor You._

Which of your qualities are you most glad God gave you?

20___

_____

_____

_____

_____

20___

_____

_____

_____

_____

20___

_____

_____

_____

_____

_____

Creator God, I am so thankful to be Your child. I might take a lifetime
to figure myself out, but I can rest in knowing that I belong to You.

If you had limo service for a week, how would you use it?

20___ _____

_____

_____

_____

_____

20___ _____

_____

_____

_____

_____

20___ _____

_____

_____

_____

_____

Help me to use every blessing for good purposes.
I want to share what I receive and enjoy it fully.

JANUARY 10

When have you felt really brave?

20___ _____

_____

_____

_____

20___ _____

_____

_____

_____

20___ _____

_____

_____

_____

_____

*God, I become bold with Your love. When I am unsure about what
to say or do, I sense Your support, guidance, and strength.*

JANUARY 11

Which chore do you wish you never had to do again?

20___

20___

20___

*Lord, help me to always be willing to serve and to
be thinking of new ways to serve others.*

JANUARY 12

What is your favorite movie?

20____

_____

20____

_____

20____

_____

God, thank You for creativity and stories.

Do you think your life is easier or harder than your
parents' lives were when they were young?

20___ _____

_____

_____

_____

20___ _____

_____

_____

_____

20___ _____

_____

_____

_____

_____

Lord, thank You for the experiences and wisdom my parents share with me.

JANUARY 14

If you could be a famous singer, actor, or explorer, which would you be?

20___ _____

20___ _____

20___ _____

God, what special abilities have You given Me? Help me to know so I can serve You and fulfill the purpose You have planned for my life.

What decision have you made lately?

20___ _____

_____

_____

_____

20___ _____

_____

_____

_____

20___ _____

_____

_____

_____

_____

"This command is a lamp, this teaching is a light, and correction
and instruction are the way to life."—PROVERBS 6:23

JANUARY 16

What are you looking forward to?

20___ _____

_____

_____

_____

20___ _____

_____

_____

_____

20___ _____

_____

_____

_____

_____

God, when I face something for the very first time, help me to remember that
You are walking right beside me. Discovering new things with You is exciting.

When have you pretended to be different than you are?

20_ _ _____

_____

_____

_____

_____

20_ _ _____

_____

_____

_____

_____

20_ _ _____

_____

_____

_____

_____

*Lord, help me to love the real me so that I reflect the
real You. I don't want to be fake with others.*

JANUARY 18

What is a typical school day like?

20___ _____

_____

_____

_____

20___ _____

_____

_____

_____

20___ _____

_____

_____

_____

_____

Jesus, I love knowing that You are with me as I learn and make friends.

JANUARY 19

When did you last laugh really, really hard?

20__ _____

_____

_____

_____

20__ _____

_____

_____

_____

20__ _____

_____

_____

_____

_____

"He will yet fill your mouth with laughter and
your lips with shouts of joy."—JOB 8:21

What would you do for a national talent contest?

20___ _____

_____

_____

_____

_____

20___ _____

_____

_____

_____

_____

20___ _____

_____

_____

_____

_____

_____

God, I praise You for everything I can do, big or small.

What is your favorite piece of clothing?

20___ _____

_____

_____

_____

20___ _____

_____

_____

_____

20___ _____

_____

_____

_____

_____

When I get dressed each morning, please help me to think
of each piece of clothing as a gift—and to thank You.

Draw a picture that represents your mood.

20___ _____

_____

_____

_____

20___ _____

_____

_____

_____

20___ _____

_____

_____

_____

Whether I am happy or sad, God, You understand me.

JANUARY 23

Which of your friends knows you the best?

20___

20___

20___

*Jesus, You shaped my heart, and You know it so well. I feel safe
knowing that nothing in my life will ever surprise You.*

JANUARY 24

What's your favorite word to use these days?

20___ _____

_____

_____

_____

20___ _____

_____

_____

_____

20___ _____

_____

_____

_____

"May these words of my mouth and this meditation of my heart be
pleasing in your sight, LORD, my Rock and my Redeemer." —PSALM 19:14

JANUARY 25

Where do you like to be when you are alone?

20__ _____

_____

_____

_____

20__ _____

_____

_____

_____

20__ _____

_____

_____

_____

_____

Lord, I am thankful that You are always right here with me. When I am by myself, I can talk to You.

Do you like to read the Bible? Why or why not?

20___ _____

_____

_____

_____

_____

20___ _____

_____

_____

_____

_____

20___ _____

_____

_____

_____

_____

*Give me a hunger for Your Word, God. Show me Your plan
for me as I dig deeper into the story of the Bible.*

JANUARY 27

Describe your feet or hands. Why are you grateful for them?

20_ _ _____

_____

_____

_____

20_ _ _____

_____

_____

_____

20_ _ _____

_____

_____

_____

_____

*I am in awe that You care about every little detail
of my life, my body, and my spirit.*

What is your favorite time with family during the week?

20__ _____
_____
_____
_____
_____

20__ _____
_____
_____
_____
_____

20__ _____
_____
_____
_____
_____

Jesus, give my family a desire and opportunities to spend time together.

God must be loving, because...

20___

_____

_____

_____

_____

20___

_____

_____

_____

20___

_____

_____

_____

_____

I am surrounded by evidence of Your love, Lord. When I get distracted,
remind me of Your gifts—like sunshine, family, and comfy blankets.

What ten words best describe you?

20____

20____

20____

Help me to see myself the way You see me, God.

What story from your life do you like to tell?

20___ _____
_____
_____
_____
_____

20___ _____
_____
_____
_____
_____

20___ _____
_____
_____
_____
_____

Jesus, thank You for the gifts of life, family, friends, and memories.

FEBRUARY 1

What would your dream bedroom makeover look like?

20___

20___

20___

God, please give me a clever mind that delights in creative expression.

FEBRUARY 2

Describe a time when it was hard to tell
the truth—but you did anyway.

20___

20___

20___

"Truthful lips endure forever, but a lying tongue
lasts only a moment."—PROVERBS 12:19

FEBRUARY 3

If you could meet Jesus when He was your
age, what would you talk to Him about?

20___ _____

_____

_____

_____

_____

20___ _____

_____

_____

_____

_____

20___ _____

_____

_____

_____

_____

*Jesus, I can talk to You about anything. I want to chat with You
every day because I have so much to tell You and ask You.*

Imagine being a famous chef. What is your specialty?

20___ ___

_____

_____

_____

_____

20___ ___

_____

_____

_____

_____

20___ ___

_____

_____

_____

_____

Every flavor, food, spice, and sweetness comes from You, God!

You are chosen to run the country for a
day. What will you make sure to do?

20___ _____

_____

_____

_____

20___ _____

_____

_____

_____

20___ _____

_____

_____

_____

_____

May everything I say and do remind people of Your grace and strength, Lord.

When have you felt shy?

20___ _____

_____

_____

_____

_____

20___ _____

_____

_____

_____

_____

20___ _____

_____

_____

_____

_____

*God, when I feel unsure, remind me that You are beside
me in every situation and every conversation.*

FEBRUARY 7

How are you similar to or different from your mom or dad?

20___ _____

_____

_____

_____

20___ _____

_____

_____

_____

20___ _____

_____

_____

_____

_____

God, each person in my family is a gift to the
others. Help us to treat each other that way.

FEBRUARY 8

What topic do you want to learn more about?

20_____ _____

_____

_____

_____

20_____ _____

_____

_____

_____

20_____ _____

_____

_____

_____

Please help me to grow in knowledge and truth.

FEBRUARY 9

Sit still for four minutes. What happened?.How did you feel?

20___

20___

20___

"Be still, and know that I am God."—PSALM 46:10

If you were a character from a book, who would you want to be?

20____ _____

20____ _____

20____ _____

Thank You, Lord, for times of play. They help me embrace possibility.

FEBRUARY 11

What is your favorite breakfast?

20___

20___

20___

I am so grateful to You for the simplest pleasures.

FEBRUARY 12

Which are you more often—clumsy or graceful?

20___ _____

_____

_____

_____

20___ _____

_____

_____

20___ _____

_____

_____

_____

Jesus, when I stumble, You pick me up and guide me forward.
When I take perfect steps, You are the one leading me.

FEBRUARY 13

The strangest thing I have seen recently is...

20___ _____

20___ _____

20___ _____

Help me to notice more and more of Your wild and wonderful world. What have I been missing? Show me, Lord.

How have you shown love to someone recently?
How has someone shown love to you?

20___ _____

_____

_____

_____

20___ _____

_____

_____

_____

20___ _____

_____

_____

_____

"A new command I give you: Love one another." —JOHN 13:34

What is something you own that is difficult for you to share?

20___

20___

20___

FEBRUARY 16

Which subject in school is your favorite?

20___ _____

_____

_____

_____

20___ _____

_____

_____

_____

20___ _____

_____

_____

_____

Lord, help me to learn things that are helpful and true.
I know You are preparing me for great things!

FEBRUARY 17

When do you feel close to God?

20___ _____

_____

_____

_____

20___ _____

_____

_____

_____

20___ _____

_____

_____

_____

_____

"Surely I am with you always, to the very end
of the age."—MATTHEW 28:20

What do you do when you can't sleep?

20_ _ _____
_____
_____
_____

20_ _ _____
_____
_____
_____

20_ _ _____
_____
_____
_____

Jesus, calm my thoughts and worries so I can rest and be healthy.

FEBRUARY 19

What do you want permission to do or be?

20___ _____

_____

_____

_____

_____

20___ _____

_____

_____

_____

_____

20___ _____

_____

_____

_____

_____

God, help me to believe in the potential You have given me.

If you were in charge of your family, what
would you have them do immediately?

20___ _____

_____

_____

_____

20___ _____

_____

_____

_____

20___ _____

_____

_____

_____

_____

Show us how to be a united and loving family, Lord.

FEBRUARY 21

When you have a spare moment, what do you usually do to fill it?

20_ _ _____

_____

_____

_____

20_ _ _____

_____

_____

_____

20_ _ _____

_____

_____

_____

"My mouth is filled with your praise, declaring
your splendor all day long."—PSALM 71:8

When have your feelings been hurt?

20__ _____

_____

_____

_____

_____

20__ _____

_____

_____

_____

20__ _____

_____

_____

_____

_____

God, I lean into Your comfort when I am sad. I feel safe by believing in You.

FEBRUARY 23

Would you rather fill a blank canvas, a blank
page, or an open piece of land?

20___ _____

_____

_____

_____

_____

20___ _____

_____

_____

_____

_____

20___ _____

_____

_____

_____

_____

Jesus, help me fill my world with good things.

Recall a recent dream. What do you think it means?

20___ _____

_____

_____

_____

20___ _____

_____

_____

_____

20___ _____

_____

_____

_____

_____

"Each of us had a dream the same night, and each dream
had a meaning of its own." —GENESIS 41:11

FEBRUARY 25

What are the most important words you said recently?

20___

20___

20___

May the words I speak honor You and lift up others. When I have the
chance to influence others, help me to point them to You, God.

FEBRUARY 26

Who is your favorite teacher?

20____ _____

_____

_____

_____

20____ _____

_____

_____

_____

20____ _____

_____

_____

_____

_____

"Guide me in your truth and teach me, for you are God my
Savior, and my hope is in you all day long."—PSALM 25:5

Who in your life needs help? How might you help them?

20___ _____

_____

_____

_____

_____

20___ _____

_____

_____

_____

_____

20___ _____

_____

_____

_____

_____

Lord, open my eyes to see how I can make a difference in someone's life.

FEBRUARY 28 AND 29

How could you pray without words?
What is the biggest leap of faith you've ever taken?

20__ _____
_____
_____
_____
_____

20__ _____
_____
_____
_____
_____

20__ _____
_____
_____
_____
_____

Let every part of my life be a prayer so I can live in Your awesome power.

You've been hired to make a commercial. What company or product would you like to promote?

20___ _____

_____

_____

_____

_____

20___ _____

_____

_____

_____

_____

20___ _____

_____

_____

_____

_____

_____

Give me wisdom, Lord, to represent You in all I do.

If you could be any animal on Noah's Ark, which animal would you be?

20___ _____

_____

_____

_____

_____

20___ _____

_____

_____

_____

_____

20___ _____

_____

_____

_____

_____

You are an amazing Creator! I love the way You used Noah to do a great thing.
Help me to always say yes to You when You ask me to put my faith into action.

MARCH 3

Who is your best friend?

20___

20___

20___

"A friend loves at all times."—PROVERBS 17:17

What was your last outdoor activity? Was it fun?

20___ _____

_____

_____

_____

20___ _____

_____

_____

_____

20___ _____

_____

_____

_____

"Let the rivers clap their hands, let the mountains
sing together for joy."—PSALM 98:8

MARCH 5

What world problem would you like to solve? How might you help solve that problem in a small way today?

20___ _____

_____

_____

_____

_____

20___ _____

_____

_____

_____

20___ _____

_____

_____

_____

_____

Jesus, use me as Your hands and heart to serve a hurting world.
Guide me to do something this week that helps others.

MARCH 6

What toppings would you put on your ideal ice cream sundae?

20____ _____
_____
_____
_____

20____ _____
_____
_____
_____

20____ _____
_____
_____
_____

God, Your goodness is even better than
chocolate and whipped cream!

What is something you have never said aloud—but wanted to?

20__ _____

_____

_____

_____

20__ _____

_____

_____

_____

20__ _____

_____

_____

_____

_____

Show me how to share my thoughts and ideas
with confidence and kindness, Lord.

MARCH 8

My heart is like a...

20__ _____

_____

_____

_____

20__ _____

_____

_____

_____

20__ _____

_____

_____

_____

"Above all else, guard your heart, for everything
you do flows from it."—PROVERBS 4:23

What is something you are willing to save money to buy?

20___ _____
_____
_____
_____

20___ _____
_____
_____
_____

20___ _____
_____
_____
_____
_____

God, show me how to be a good steward of
the blessings You provide.

MARCH 10

What unites your family?

20___ _____

_____

_____

_____

20___ _____

_____

_____

_____

20___ _____

_____

_____

_____

_____

*Thank You for my family, Lord. Watch over us and connect
our hearts. Help us to be patient with one another.*

MARCH 11

What is your favorite public place (library,
church, concert hall, school, park…)?

20_ _ _____

_____

_____

_____

20_ _ _____

_____

_____

_____

20_ _ _____

_____

_____

_____

_____

Jesus, I love being able to talk to You anywhere.
There is no wrong place to pray!

When did you *not* speak up and later wish you had?

20___ _____

_____

_____

_____

20___ _____

_____

_____

_____

20___ _____

_____

_____

_____

_____

Lord, give me courage to use my voice and influence for good purposes.

MARCH 13

Are you more like a poem, a book, a riddle, or a song?

20___

20___

20___

Jesus, today I celebrate how You created me to be unique. I
want to see Your goodness in who I am and what I do.

What would be an encouraging theme or motto for this month?

20___

_____

_____

_____

_____

20___

_____

_____

_____

_____

20___

_____

_____

_____

_____

_____

"Fix these words of mine in your hearts and
minds." —DEUTERONOMY 11:18

Whom do you wish you could talk to face-to-face?

20___ _____

_____

_____

_____

20___ _____

_____

_____

_____

20___ _____

_____

_____

_____

_____

When I pray, I feel as if we're eye to eye...or maybe heart to heart.

MARCH 16

Do you learn best by watching, reading, hearing, or doing?

20___

20___

20___

"Whatever you have learned or received or heard from me, or
seen in me—put it into practice."—PHILIPPIANS 4:9

When you blow out a birthday candle or discover
a four-leaf clover, what do you wish for?

20___ _____

_____

_____

_____

_____

20___ _____

_____

_____

_____

_____

20___ _____

_____

_____

_____

_____

God, may You always be the one who shapes who I am and what I hope for.

What question do you have for your mom or dad?

20_ _ _____

_____

_____

_____

_____

20_ _ _____

_____

_____

_____

_____

20_ _ _____

_____

_____

_____

_____

Jesus, help me to understand more about You from my parents.

MARCH 19

When have you been jealous?

20___

20___

20___

*Help me not to envy others but to be happy with
myself and the blessings You give me.*

MARCH 20

You've joined the circus!
What is your act?

20_ _ _____

_____

_____

_____

20_ _ _____

_____

_____

_____

20_ _ _____

_____

_____

_____

God, reveal to me my abilities big and small, serious and silly.

Do you tend to be quiet or more vocal? Has that changed?

20____ _____

_____

_____

_____

20____ _____

_____

_____

_____

20____ _____

_____

_____

_____

_____

*Help me to speak out when I need to, Lord, and
teach me to be quiet when that is best.*

MARCH 22

If you could change your name, what would you change it to?

20__ _____

_____

_____

_____

20__ _____

_____

_____

_____

20__ _____

_____

_____

_____

_____

Jesus, may I always bring honor to Your name.

Would you rather live in a treehouse or on a houseboat?

20___ _____

_____

_____

_____

20___ _____

_____

_____

_____

20___ _____

_____

_____

_____

_____

"Anyone who loves me will obey my teaching. My Father will love them,
and we will come to them and make our home with them."—JOHN 14:23

MARCH 29

Do you collect anything?
If you were to start collecting something, what would it be?

20__ _____

_____

_____

_____

20__ _____

_____

_____

_____

20__ _____

_____

_____

_____

Lord, help me collect wisdom and good friends.

MARCH 25

How have you experienced God's love this week?

20___ _____
_____
_____
_____
_____

20___ _____
_____
_____
_____
_____

20___ _____
_____
_____
_____
_____

May I never go a day without sharing Your love with others, Lord.

MARCH 26

Which subject in school is most challenging?

20___ _____

_____

_____

_____

_____

20___ _____

_____

_____

_____

_____

20___ _____

_____

_____

_____

_____

*Please give me patience and a clear mind to
learn...even when it doesn't come easily.*

MARCH 27

What is your favorite spring activity?

20___ _____

_____

_____

_____

20___ _____

_____

_____

_____

20___ _____

_____

_____

_____

_____

Spring flowers remind me that You make all things new.

Would you rather be able to read people's
hearts or their minds? Why?

20___

_____

_____

_____

_____

20___

_____

_____

_____

_____

20___

_____

_____

_____

_____

_____

God, show me how to give my attention to the people you bring into my life.

Describe the color green.

20___ _____

_____

_____

_____

_____

20___ _____

_____

_____

_____

_____

20___ _____

_____

_____

_____

_____

Today I will notice the many miracles of Your creation.

What do you want to invent?

20___ _____
_____
_____
_____

20___ _____
_____
_____
_____

20___ _____
_____
_____
_____

When my thoughts get stuck on "I can't," remind me
of what is possible in Your power, Lord.

If you couldn't use an electronic device of any kind for two weeks,
how would you feel? How would you use your extra time?

20___ _____

_____

_____

_____

_____

20___ _____

_____

_____

_____

20___ _____

_____

_____

_____

_____

"I want you to do whatever will help you serve the Lord best,
with as few distractions as possible."—1 CORINTHIANS 7:35 NLT

When have you felt embarrassed or foolish?

20___ _____

20___ _____

20___ _____

*God, when I make a mistake, remind me of Your
love, acceptance, and forgiveness.*

Which part of the Easter story do you think is the most amazing?

20___ _____

_____

_____

_____

20___ _____

_____

_____

_____

20___ _____

_____

_____

_____

_____

Jesus, Your resurrection reminds me of Your power to
transform my heart and give me new life.

If you could be a grown-up for a week, what would you do?

20___ _____

_____

_____

_____

_____

20___ _____

_____

_____

_____

_____

20___ _____

_____

_____

_____

_____

_____

Show me how to be responsible and to follow the path You have for me, Lord.

What is your favorite song? Write down your favorite line.

20__ _____

_____

_____

_____

20__ _____

_____

_____

_____

20__ _____

_____

_____

_____

_____

"Sing to the LORD a new song." —PSALM 98:1

When have you surprised yourself?

20___ _____

_____

_____

_____

20___ _____

_____

_____

_____

20___ _____

_____

_____

_____

God, give me eyes to see how You are changing me and increasing my faith.

I am glad that God is bigger than...

20__ _____

20__ _____

20__ _____

Jesus, today I am handing over to You a specific worry that I have been carrying around. Thank You for giving me peace.

APRIL 7

What superpower do you wish you had?

20__ _____

_____

_____

_____

20__ _____

_____

_____

_____

20__ _____

_____

_____

_____

"I can do all this through him who gives me strength."—PHILIPPIANS 4:13

APRIL 8

When have you felt listened to?
Who listens to you?

20___ _____

_____

_____

_____

20___ _____

_____

_____

_____

20___ _____

_____

_____

_____

_____

Jesus, I am grateful for the caring, supportive people You bring into my life.

APRIL 9

How do you cheer up your brother, sister, or friend?

20____

20____

20____

"Encourage one another and build each other up, just as
in fact you are doing."—1 THESSALONIANS 5:11

What can you do now that you couldn't
do when you were younger?

20___ _____

_____

_____

_____

_____

20___ _____

_____

_____

_____

_____

20___ _____

_____

_____

_____

_____

Lord, as I mature, help me to grow more like You.

What do you like or dislike about church?

20___ _____

_____

_____

_____

_____

20___ _____

_____

_____

_____

_____

20___ _____

_____

_____

_____

_____

Jesus, when I am with those who follow You,
help us to be the family you made us to be.

What nickname do you want?

20___ _____

_____

_____

_____

20___ _____

_____

_____

_____

20___ _____

_____

_____

_____

Abba, El Shaddai, Yahweh...I love learning Your names
and what they reveal about You, God.

What challenge have you and your family faced together?

20__ _____

_____

_____

_____

_____

20__ _____

_____

_____

_____

20__ _____

_____

_____

_____

_____

Thank You, Jesus, for strengthening my family
through good times and difficult times.

Bonus: What question do you want to answer today?

20___ _____

_____

_____

_____

20___ _____

_____

_____

_____

20___ _____

_____

_____

_____

"Ask and it will be given to you; seek and you will find; knock
and the door will be opened to you."—MATTHEW 7:7

APRIL 15

What would you like to build?

20___ _____

_____

_____

_____

20___ _____

_____

_____

_____

20___ _____

_____

_____

_____

The sky is the limit when I place my wishes and dreams in Your hands.

Do you prefer sweet, sour, or salty?

20___ _____

_____

_____

_____

20___ _____

_____

_____

_____

20___ _____

_____

_____

_____

"Taste and see that the LORD is good; blessed is the
one who takes refuge in him."—PSALM 34:8

You've climbed a tall mountain, and now you're leaving a note for the next person who reaches the top. What will you write?

20___

20___

20___

Jesus, thank You for a faith that reaches the highest heights. I want to share it with the world.

What is the best idea you've had lately?

20___

20___

20___

My inspiration comes from You, God. Lead me, and I will follow.

What have you lost that was important to you?

20___ _____

_____

_____

_____

20___ _____

_____

_____

_____

20___ _____

_____

_____

_____

_____

Lord, thank You for never losing track of me.

What is your favorite way to spend a weekend?

20___ _____

_____

_____

_____

20___ _____

_____

_____

_____

20___ _____

_____

_____

_____

_____

Because of You, Jesus, each day is a chance to explore
the wonders of creation, friendships, and ideas.

When and how has someone made you feel included?

20__ __ _____

_____

_____

_____

20__ __ _____

_____

_____

_____

20__ __ _____

_____

_____

_____

"Rise up; this matter is in your hands. We will support
you, so take courage and do it." —EZRA 10:4

APRIL 22

What is something scary that you want God
to protect you from or help you with?

20____ _____

_____

_____

_____

20____ _____

_____

_____

_____

20____ _____

_____

_____

_____

_____

*Lord, You see me when I am intimidated and scared. Help me to feel
Your presence when I feel afraid and when I face new challenges.*

Who can make you laugh, even when you don't want to?

20___ _____

_____

_____

_____

_____

20___ _____

_____

_____

_____

_____

20___ _____

_____

_____

_____

_____

Thank You for people who cause joy to bubble up from my soul.

How do you get ready for bed?

20___ _____
_____
_____
_____

20___ _____
_____
_____
_____

20___ _____
_____
_____
_____
_____

*God, help me to see each day as a blessing. Thank You
for restoring my body and mind while I sleep.*

What is the most important thing in a friendship?

20__ __

20__ __

20__ __

"Dear friends, let us love one another, for love
comes from God."—1 JOHN 4:7

APRIL 26

Would you rather go camping or stay in a hotel?

20___

20___

20___

*Wherever I am, You are with me, Lord. And wherever I
rest my head, You are watching over me.*

APRIL 27

Which fruit of the Spirit is strongest in your life?

20___ _____

_____

_____

_____

20___ _____

_____

_____

_____

20___ _____

_____

_____

_____

_____

"The fruit of the Spirit is love, joy, peace, patience, kindness, goodness, faithfulness, gentleness, self-control."—GALATIANS 5:22-23 NASB

APRIL 28

French fries, mashed potatoes, or hash browns?

20___ _____

20___ _____

20___ _____

Jesus, thank You for simple pleasures and silly choices that make me happy.

A movie is being made about your life! What
famous actor should play you?

20__ _____

_____

_____

_____

_____

20__ _____

_____

_____

_____

_____

20__ _____

_____

_____

_____

_____

God, I pray that others will see Your grace at work in my life.

APRIL 30

Who helps you know and understand Jesus?

20___ _____

_____

_____

_____

20___ _____

_____

_____

_____

20___ _____

_____

_____

_____

God, when I witness someone who is strong in faith,
give me the wisdom to learn from them.

MAY 1

Would you rather sail across the ocean on a ship
or soar above the plains in a hot-air balloon?

20___ _____

_____

_____

_____

20___ _____

_____

_____

_____

20___ _____

_____

_____

_____

_____

Jesus, You have invited me on a journey of faith.
This is the greatest adventure of all.

Your classroom is ready and waiting—what are you teaching?

20___ _____

_____

_____

_____

_____

20___ _____

_____

_____

_____

_____

20___ _____

_____

_____

_____

_____

"Don't let anyone look down on you because you are young,
but set an example for the believers in speech, in conduct,
in love, in faith and in purity."—1 TIMOTHY 4:12

What do you wish you could remember better?

20___ _____
_____
_____
_____
_____

20___ _____
_____
_____
_____
_____

20___ _____
_____
_____
_____
_____

God, help me to always be thankful for the
people, places, and experiences of my life.

MAY 4

What is one thing you think God wants you to do this week?

20___

20___

20___

"Since you are my rock and my fortress, for the sake
of your name lead and guide me."—PSALM 31:3

MAY 5

My perfect day would include...

20__ _____

_____

_____

_____

_____

20__ _____

_____

_____

_____

_____

20__ _____

_____

_____

_____

_____

God, don't ever let me settle for less than You have planned for me!

Draw the logo of your brand.

20___

20___

20___

Lord, You are the master designer. Create a work of beauty in and through me.

What is your prayer today?

20___ _____
_____
_____
_____

20___ _____
_____
_____
_____

20___ _____
_____
_____
_____

Jesus, I love You.

What important qualities do you want in a close friend?

20___ _____

_____

_____

_____

_____

20___ _____

_____

_____

_____

_____

20___ _____

_____

_____

_____

_____

*God, give me the desire to see the best in people and to
spend time with those who seek their best in You.*

Do you prefer to twirl, roll, run, skip, or recline?

20___ _____

_____

_____

_____

20___ _____

_____

_____

_____

20___ _____

_____

_____

_____

_____

I am grateful for the many ways my body can move.

MAY 10

What mistake did you make recently?

20___ _____

_____

_____

_____

20___ _____

_____

_____

_____

20___ _____

_____

_____

_____

Lord, thank You for forgiving me when I goof up. Show me how to make things right and to receive Your grace with gladness.

MAY 11

What do you wish people understood about you?

20__ _____

20__ _____

20__ _____

"You have searched me, LORD, and you know me. You know when I sit
and when I rise; you perceive my thoughts from afar."—PSALM 139:1-2

Which musical instrument represents your
personality? Drum? Flute? Piano? Gong?

20___ _____

_____

_____

_____

_____

20___ _____

_____

_____

_____

_____

20___ _____

_____

_____

_____

_____

May my life be like a song that makes You happy, God.

MAY 13

If you could declare a national holiday, what would
your day celebrate, and what would you call it?

20___

20___

20___

Jesus, when I get too serious, please help me have fun with
You. You have given me so much to be happy about!

MAY 19

What is your greatest strength?

20___ _____

_____

_____

_____

_____

20___ _____

_____

_____

_____

20___ _____

_____

_____

_____

_____

God, I am still discovering the ways that I am unique and strong.
Teach me more about who I am and who I can become.

MAY 15

What is your favorite Bible verse or story?

20___ _____

_____

_____

_____

_____

20___ _____

_____

_____

_____

_____

20___ _____

_____

_____

_____

_____

God, help me to understand the Bible and to learn
more about Your faithfulness and strength.

MAY 16

When have you put someone else's needs ahead of your own?

20__ _____

_____

_____

_____

20__ _____

_____

_____

_____

20__ _____

_____

_____

_____

"Learn to do right; seek justice. Defend the oppressed. Take up the cause of the fatherless; plead the case of the widow."—ISAIAH 1:17

MAY 17

Do you ever have something important to say
but choose to be quiet instead? If so, why?

20___ _____

_____

_____

_____

_____

20___ _____

_____

_____

_____

_____

20___ _____

_____

_____

_____

_____

God, please help me not to be afraid to share my ideas and faith.

If you could design a school building, what would it look like?

20___

_____

_____

_____

_____

20___

_____

_____

_____

_____

20___

_____

_____

_____

_____

Lord, help me to learn quickly and to share my knowledge.

What kind of car or vehicle do you like?

20___ _____
_____
_____
_____

20___ _____
_____
_____
_____

20___ _____
_____
_____
_____

"Say to Daughter Zion, 'See, your king comes to you, gentle and riding on a donkey, and on a colt, the foal of a donkey.'"—MATTHEW 21:5

What is your prayer for your family?

20___ _____

20___ _____

20___ _____

God, thank You for watching over my family. Help us to support one another and to share Your love with others.

MAY 21

Is meeting new people difficult or easy for you? Why?

20_ _ _____

_____

_____

_____

20_ _ _____

_____

_____

_____

20_ _ _____

_____

_____

_____

_____

*Help me to make a new friend this year, Jesus—and
to treat everyone with respect and kindness.*

If you had to start working tomorrow, what job would you want?

20___ _____

_____

_____

_____

20___ _____

_____

_____

_____

20___ _____

_____

_____

_____

"Whatever you do, work at it with all your heart, as working
for the Lord, not for human masters."—COLOSSIANS 3:23

What makes you cry?

20_ _ _____

_____

_____

_____

_____

20_ _ _____

_____

_____

_____

20_ _ _____

_____

_____

_____

_____

Jesus, You know when my heart hurts. I trust You to comfort and help me.

Fruit of the Spirit question: How do you express love?

20__ _____

_____

_____

_____

_____

20__ _____

_____

_____

_____

_____

20__ _____

_____

_____

_____

_____

"Love does not delight in evil but rejoices with the
truth. It always protects, always trusts, always hopes,
always perseveres." —1 CORINTHIANS 13:6-7

When you daydream, what do you think about?

20___ _____
_____
_____
_____
_____

20___ _____
_____
_____
_____
_____

20___ _____
_____
_____
_____
_____
_____

Give me a hope and a dream, Lord. I will follow the path You lay out for me.

Has someone you loved died?

20___ _____

_____

_____

_____

20___ _____

_____

_____

_____

20___ _____

_____

_____

_____

_____

*Lord, it is so hard to lose someone. I feel better when I
remember that You care for us all and hold us close.*

Who is the oldest person you know? The youngest?

20__ _____

_____

_____

_____

20__ _____

_____

_____

_____

20__ _____

_____

_____

_____

"The plans of the LORD stand firm forever, the purposes
of his heart through all generations."—PSALM 33:11

What would you miss most if you had to leave
behind your belongings, home, and school?

20___ _____

_____

_____

_____

_____

20___ _____

_____

_____

_____

20___ _____

_____

_____

_____

_____

*Jesus, I am grateful for all the treasures You have given me. The greatest
of all is Your presence in my life, and that cannot ever be taken away.*

What activity or hobby do you want to try this year?

20__ _____
_____
_____
_____

20__ _____
_____
_____
_____

20__ _____
_____
_____
_____
_____

Give me a spirit of adventure and a willingness to try and to try again if I fail.

What do you miss about being younger?

20__ _____
_____
_____
_____

20__ _____
_____
_____
_____

20__ _____
_____
_____
_____

"Truly I tell you, anyone who will not receive the kingdom
of God like a little child will never enter it."—LUKE 18:17

MAY 31

What is your favorite day of the week? Why?

20___ _____
_____
_____
_____
_____

20___ _____
_____
_____
_____
_____

20___ _____
_____
_____
_____
_____

*Jesus, when I wake up each morning, I will give
thanks for the gift of a new day.*

JUNE 1

Do you want to be a parent someday? Why or why not?

20__ _____

_____

_____

_____

20__ _____

_____

_____

_____

20__ _____

_____

_____

_____

Lord, show me how to grow into an adult who will be
a good example as a mentor or as a parent.

JUNE 2

What activity or craft would you be willing to
practice daily in order to get really good at it?

20____ _____

_____

_____

_____

20____ _____

_____

_____

_____

20____ _____

_____

_____

_____

_____

God, I want to have a disciplined heart and give my all to bring glory to You.

JUNE 3

When do you lose track of time?

20___ _____
_____
_____
_____

20___ _____
_____
_____
_____

20___ _____
_____
_____
_____

Thank You, Lord, for helping me to include joy and laughter in each day.

What four words describe your home?

20___ _____

_____

_____

_____

20___ _____

_____

_____

_____

20___ _____

_____

_____

_____

"As for me and my household, we will serve the LORD."—JOSHUA 24:15

JUNE 5

Which of your friends is the most different from you?

20___ _____

_____

_____

_____

20___ _____

_____

_____

_____

20___ _____

_____

_____

_____

Jesus, I love how unique each one of my friends is. You made every person to be special and loved.

JUNE 6

What would your ultimate party be like,
and whom would you invite?

20___

20___

20___

You have been so good to my family and me—help me to celebrate every day!

JUNE 7

If you could go back in time, which Bible event
or story would you want to experience?

20___ _____

_____

_____

_____

20___ _____

_____

_____

_____

20___ _____

_____

_____

_____

_____

"I have written to you who are young in the faith because you
are strong. God's word lives in your hearts, and you have
won your battle with the evil one."—1 JOHN 2:14 NLT

When have you given away something you
cared about? How did it feel?

20___

_____

_____

_____

_____

20___

_____

_____

_____

_____

20___

_____

_____

_____

_____

_____

Lord, You know when I give from the heart and when I give
reluctantly. Help me to serve others happily and often.

If you tried to set a world record, what would you do?

20___ _____

_____

_____

_____

20___ _____

_____

_____

_____

20___ _____

_____

_____

_____

_____

*Every day is an opportunity to discover more about
how You made me, God. It's an adventure!*

JUNE 10

Your life is an awesome gift from God.
How would you like to use it?

20___ _____

20___ _____

20___ _____

Lord, this life I have is an awesome gift. Help me to make
the most of it by living with honor and integrity.

What is the nicest compliment you've ever received?

20___ _____

_____

_____

_____

_____

20___ _____

_____

_____

_____

20___ _____

_____

_____

_____

_____

"Gracious words are a honeycomb, sweet to the soul
and healing to the bones."—PROVERBS 16:24

When and where do you feel the safest?

20___ _____

_____

_____

_____

20___ _____

_____

_____

_____

20___ _____

_____

_____

_____

When I cry out to You, God, You help me feel safe and secure.

JUNE 13

What club are you a part of? What club would you like to join?

20___ _____

20___ _____

20___ _____

God, guide me to people who will understand
what is important to me and who share my passions.

JUNE 19

What do you want to start?

20___ _____

_____

_____

_____

20___ _____

_____

_____

_____

20___ _____

_____

_____

_____

_____

You always walk beside me and guide me, so I know I
can start something new with confidence.

When have you felt lonely?

20___ _____

_____

_____

_____

20___ _____

_____

_____

_____

20___ _____

_____

_____

_____

"Never will I leave you;
never will I forsake you."—HEBREWS 13:5

JUNE 16

Which do you like better—eating at home or at restaurants?

20___

20___

20___

Wherever I eat and drink, may I always give thanks to
You for providing enough food and nourishment.

What fact about you might surprise most of your friends?

20___ _____

_____

_____

_____

20___ _____

_____

_____

_____

20___ _____

_____

_____

_____

Jesus, You know me better than anyone else.
This truth makes me feel good.

JUNE 18

What is your favorite silly thing to do?

20_ _ _____
_____
_____
_____

20_ _ _____
_____
_____
_____

20_ _ _____
_____
_____
_____
_____

"Then young women will dance and be glad, young men and old as well. I will turn their mourning into gladness." —JEREMIAH 31:13

God has given you special gifts.
How can you use them to make the world a better place?

20___ _____

_____

_____

_____

20___ _____

_____

_____

_____

20___ _____

_____

_____

_____

_____

*Open my eyes, Lord, and show me how I can step
up, speak up, and show up in the world.*

JUNE 20

What do you like about having or not having siblings?

20___ _____

_____

_____

_____

20___ _____

_____

_____

_____

20___ _____

_____

_____

_____

*Lord, fill my heart with gratitude for
the family You have given me.*

What is your favorite summer activity?

20__ _____

_____

_____

_____

20__ _____

_____

_____

_____

20__ _____

_____

_____

_____

There is so much to enjoy and
have fun with under Your sun, God.

JUNE 22

If you could be invisible for a full day, what would you do?

20___

20___

20___

*Lord, I am never invisible to You. Your grace covers
me, and You watch over me as a loving Father.*

JUNE 23

Do you have a pet? What animal would
you like to have for a new pet?

20___ _____

_____

_____

_____

_____

20___ _____

_____

_____

_____

_____

20___ _____

_____

_____

_____

_____

Your creatures fill me with wonder and make me
want to praise You all the more, God.

Fruit of the Spirit question: When have
you shared joy with others?

20___ _____

_____

_____

_____

_____

20___ _____

_____

_____

_____

_____

20___ _____

_____

_____

_____

_____

*Help me to start a movement of joy in
my school and neighborhood, Lord.*

JUNE 25

I love...

20_____ _____

_____

_____

_____

_____

20_____ _____

_____

_____

_____

_____

20_____ _____

_____

_____

_____

_____

Jesus, You have an endless supply of love. Thank You for
sharing it with me and helping me to spread it to others.

JUNE 26

What is your favorite smell?

20___ _____
_____
_____
_____

20___ _____
_____
_____
_____

20___ _____
_____
_____
_____
_____

"We are to God the pleasing aroma of Christ among those who are
being saved and those who are perishing."—2 CORINTHIANS 2:15

What is your favorite way to exercise?

20___ _____
_____
_____
_____

20___ _____
_____
_____
_____

20___ _____
_____
_____
_____
_____

Thank You for giving me the ability to stretch and build
muscles, Lord. I want to have a strong spirit and body.

If you had a tattoo on your face, what would it look like?

20___ _____

_____

_____

_____

_____

20___ _____

_____

_____

_____

20___ _____

_____

_____

_____

_____

Jesus, what do friends and strangers think is important
to me? Please let my faith be obvious to all.

Jesus says that when you help or visit the sick and needy, you are helping Him. When have you helped Him recently?

20__ _____

_____

_____

_____

_____

20__ _____

_____

_____

_____

_____

20__ _____

_____

_____

_____

_____

"Truly I tell you, whatever you did for one of the least of these brothers and sisters of mine, you did for me."—MATTHEW 25:40

JUNE 30

What feels impossible to do?

20___ _____

_____

_____

_____

20___ _____

_____

_____

_____

20___ _____

_____

_____

_____

_____

I believe that all things are possible in You, Lord. Remind me of this
when I feel too weak or young or insignificant to make a difference.

Where do you like to shop?

20___ _____

_____

_____

_____

20___ _____

_____

_____

_____

20___ _____

_____

_____

_____

_____

Lord, I have been given so much. Please help me
to use it wisely—to use it for good.

What is your favorite book?

20_____ _____

_____

_____

_____

20_____ _____

_____

_____

_____

20_____ _____

_____

_____

_____

Lord, please help me to have creative ideas,
clear thoughts, and a caring heart.

JULY 3

When have you been a good listener?

20__ _____

_____

_____

_____

20__ _____

_____

_____

_____

20__ _____

_____

_____

_____

_____

God, when I get tired of listening, remind me how much it hurts my feelings when people ignore me. Give me the sincere desire to be a good listener.

JULY 4

Why does freedom matter?

20__ _____

20__ _____

20__ _____

*God, You have given me freedom to make so many
choices. Help me to respect other people's choices.*

JULY 5

If you lived in the Garden of Eden now,
what would you do all day?

20___ _____

_____

_____

_____

_____

20___ _____

_____

_____

_____

_____

20___ _____

_____

_____

_____

_____

God, help me to appreciate everything You provide,
including Your words of truth and Your guidance.

What kind of adventure do you want to have someday?

20_ _ _____
_____
_____
_____
_____

20_ _ _____
_____
_____
_____
_____

20_ _ _____
_____
_____
_____
_____

"Have you journeyed to the springs of the sea or walked
in the recesses of the deep?" —JOB 38:16

When has someone in your family stood up for you?

20__

_____

_____

_____

_____

20__

_____

_____

_____

20__

_____

_____

_____

_____

_____

Jesus, I need You and the people around me. Sometimes life is hard. It just is. Thank You that I am not supposed to handle it all by myself.

What is your favorite piece of furniture?

20___

_____
_____
_____
_____

20___

_____
_____
_____
_____

20___

_____
_____
_____
_____

When I need to sit or sleep, You provide me with a place to rest. Sometimes the simplest blessings are the most important—thank You!

JULY 9

What are you absolutely sure of?

20___ _____

_____

_____

_____

20___ _____

_____

_____

_____

20___ _____

_____

_____

_____

God, thank You that I don't have to know everything. But help me to ask
good questions and learn new things every day. You know everything!

Which animated character would you like to hang out with on a Saturday afternoon? Which one would you like to be?

20___ _____

_____

_____

_____

_____

20___ _____

_____

_____

_____

20___ _____

_____

_____

_____

_____

*It is so cool that You invented playfulness and
joy. You think of everything, God.*

What is your most frequent prayer?

20___ _____
_____
_____
_____
_____

20___ _____
_____
_____
_____
_____

20___ _____
_____
_____
_____
_____
_____

Jesus, You know what I need even before I ask. Still, You listen carefully to every word I say when I ask You for something. Thank You for caring so much.

What do you wish you could do over?

20___ _____

_____

_____

_____

_____

20___ _____

_____

_____

_____

_____

20___ _____

_____

_____

_____

_____

*God, thank You for Your forgiveness and for
showing me the right way to try again.*

Someone is writing a book about your
life. What should the title be?

20___ _____

_____

_____

_____

_____

20___ _____

_____

_____

_____

_____

20___ _____

_____

_____

_____

_____

*You are the Author of my life, Lord. I want to
partner with You to make it a great story!*

JULY 14

What are you not sure about?

20___ _____

20___ _____

20___ _____

*I have so many questions, Jesus. I'm glad You never
get tired of hearing me ask for advice.*

JULY 15

If you could go climb anything, what would you climb?

20__ __ _____

_____

_____

_____

20__ __ _____

_____

_____

_____

20__ __ _____

_____

_____

_____

_____

"[Zacchaeus] wanted to see who Jesus was, but because he was short he could not see over the crowd. So he ran ahead and climbed a sycamore-fig tree to see him, since Jesus was coming that way." —LUKE 19:3-4

JULY 16

The funniest thing I said or thought lately was...

20__ _____

_____

_____

_____

20__ _____

_____

_____

_____

20__ _____

_____

_____

_____

_____

Jesus, do You laugh with me?
I believe You are the Lord of joy.

Have you ever been bullied or picked on? When?

20___ _____

_____

_____

_____

_____

20___ _____

_____

_____

_____

_____

20___ _____

_____

_____

_____

_____

_____

God, show me how to respond when others pick on me.
Thank You for protecting my heart and reminding
me that I am of great value to You.

What is something really important that most adults forget?

20_ _ _____

_____

_____

_____

20_ _ _____

_____

_____

_____

20_ _ _____

_____

_____

_____

_____

Please help my parents remember
what it is like to be my age.

When have you felt compassion for someone
and wanted to help them?

20___ _____

_____

_____

_____

_____

20___ _____

_____

_____

_____

_____

20___ _____

_____

_____

_____

_____

"Be completely humble and gentle; be patient, bearing
with one another in love."—EPHESIANS 4:2

Fruit of the Spirit question: How could you
help other people feel peaceful?

20___ _____

_____

_____

_____

20___ _____

_____

_____

_____

20___ _____

_____

_____

_____

_____

*Jesus, may my friends enjoy peace in their
relationships with You and with each other.*

What have you been putting off that you need to do soon?

20___ _____

_____

_____

_____

_____

20___ _____

_____

_____

_____

_____

20___ _____

_____

_____

_____

_____

_____

Lord, help me to complete a task in front of me. I want to experience the satisfaction of a job well done.

How do you like to use your imagination?

20___ _____

_____

_____

_____

20___ _____

_____

_____

_____

20___ _____

_____

_____

_____

_____

"Now to him who is able to do immeasurably more than all we ask or imagine, according to his power that is at work within us, to him be glory in the church and in Christ Jesus throughout all generations, for ever and ever! Amen."—EPHESIANS 3:20-21

JULY 23

How do you like to praise God?

20___ _____

_____

_____

_____

20___ _____

_____

_____

_____

20___ _____

_____

_____

_____

_____

Jesus, may my thoughts, my words, and my actions bring You praise.

JULY 24

You're stranded on a deserted island. Who are
two people you want to be with you?

20___ _____

_____

_____

_____

20___ _____

_____

_____

_____

20___ _____

_____

_____

_____

_____

God, thank You for the friends and family You've
given me and for the help they provide.

What family story do you love to hear again and again?

20___ _____

_____

_____

_____

_____

20___ _____

_____

_____

_____

_____

20___ _____

_____

_____

_____

_____

The story of my family is part of my faith story. The good times and the hard times are all parts of my journey with You, Lord.

JULY 26

What rule do you like? What rule do you dislike?

20__ _____

_____

_____

_____

20__ _____

_____

_____

_____

20__ _____

_____

_____

_____

"These rules are only shadows of the reality yet to come. And
Christ himself is that reality."—COLOSSIANS 2:17 NLT

If you were to give an acceptance speech at an
award show, whom would you thank?

20___ _____

_____

_____

_____

_____

20___ _____

_____

_____

_____

_____

20___ _____

_____

_____

_____

_____

Everywhere I turn, You provide people who can help me in some way.
Thank You, Jesus, for leading me to them and for always being with me.

Are you the sun, the moon, or the earth?

20_____ _____

_____

_____

_____

_____

20_____ _____

_____

_____

_____

_____

20_____ _____

_____

_____

_____

_____

God, You have created every star, every planet, every moon.
We stare in awe at them, but they bow down to You.

What is your favorite board game?

20___

_____
_____
_____
_____

20___

_____
_____
_____
_____

20___

_____
_____
_____
_____
_____

Lord, please teach me how to be a good winner and a good loser.

What is one thing you want your future self
to remember about your life now?

20__ __ _____

_____

_____

_____

20__ __ _____

_____

_____

_____

20__ __ _____

_____

_____

_____

"Remember how the LORD your God led you
all the way."—DEUTERONOMY 8:2

What state or country would you like to visit?

20___ _____

_____

_____

_____

20___ _____

_____

_____

_____

20___ _____

_____

_____

_____

*You are with me wherever I go, so I look forward to exploring
new places. Give me the courage and opportunity to
see more of the world You have created, Lord.*

AUGUST 1

What possession means the most to you?

20____ _____

_____

_____

_____

_____

20____ _____

_____

_____

_____

_____

20____ _____

_____

_____

_____

_____

_____

Lord, help me to know which things are important and which things aren't. May I always value people more than possessions.

A rainbow is a symbol of God's promises. What
is one promise God has kept to you?

20__ _____

_____

_____

_____

20__ _____

_____

_____

_____

20__ _____

_____

_____

_____

_____

"I have set my rainbow in the clouds, and it will be the sign of
the covenant between me and the earth."—GENESIS 9:13

When have you felt close to your family?

20___ _____

_____

_____

_____

20___ _____

_____

_____

_____

20___ _____

_____

_____

_____

_____

God, please give my family more fun times together. Help us to appreciate each other.

What do you wish you could forget?

20___ _____

_____

_____

_____

20___ _____

_____

_____

_____

20___ _____

_____

_____

_____

_____

Lord, when painful memories come to my mind, please give me Your peace.

I can't stand...

20__ _____

_____

_____

_____

20__ _____

_____

_____

_____

20__ _____

_____

_____

_____

_____

*I want to be bold, Jesus. When people hurt each other, help
me to be part of the answer and not part of the problem.*

AUGUST 6

What do you like most about being you?

20__ _____

_____

_____

_____

20__ _____

_____

_____

_____

20__ _____

_____

_____

_____

Jesus, I am quick to see other people's strengths, but I don't always recognize my own. Show me what You love about me.

What is your favorite food?

20___

20___

20___

Everything I enjoy comes from You, God. I benefit from
nature, food, sunshine, and other simple joys You provide.

Which subject in school is the easiest for you?

20_ _

20_ _

20_ _

God, I praise You for good times and for the gift of knowledge.

AUGUST 9

Where do you want to go to college or work someday?

20__ _____

_____

_____

_____

20__ _____

_____

_____

_____

20__ _____

_____

_____

_____

*You hold my future in Your hands, Lord. I can't wait
to see what You have dreamed for me.*

Are you a cat, a dog, or a turtle?

20___ _____

_____

_____

_____

_____

20___ _____

_____

_____

_____

_____

20___ _____

_____

_____

_____

_____

God, thanks for making me the way You did. Even though I am like
my family members in some ways, I am 100 percent unique.

When did you say something you wish you hadn't said?

20___

20___

20___

Forgive me, Jesus, for sometimes speaking before I think.
Help me to avoid hurting others or causing troubles.

AUGUST 12

What would you tell a friend are your three
favorite things about Jesus?

20__ _____

_____

_____

_____

20__ _____

_____

_____

_____

20__ _____

_____

_____

_____

*Your goodness gives me a lot to talk about. Help me to always be
comfortable sharing about my friendship with You, Jesus.*

Is there anything you wish you could change about yourself?

20___

20___

20___

"I praise you because I am fearfully and wonderfully made; your works are wonderful, I know that full well."—PSALM 139:14

AUGUST 14

What do you waste a lot of?

20__ _____
_____
_____
_____
_____

20__ _____
_____
_____
_____
_____

20__ _____
_____
_____
_____
_____

*God, each blessing from You is of great value. I pray
that I won't ever squander any of them.*

AUGUST 15

When are you at your best?

20___ _____

_____

_____

_____

_____

20___ _____

_____

_____

_____

_____

20___ _____

_____

_____

_____

_____

"Do your best to present yourself to God as one approved,
a worker who does not need to be ashamed and who
correctly handles the word of truth."—2 TIMOTHY 2:15

AUGUST 16

What is the funniest thing you've heard lately?

20___ _____

_____

_____

_____

20___ _____

_____

_____

_____

20___ _____

_____

_____

_____

_____

*God, help me to notice and celebrate everything
around me that is happy and fun.*

If you were stuck in a museum for a
weekend, what would you do?

20__ _____

_____

_____

_____

20__ _____

_____

_____

_____

20__ _____

_____

_____

_____

_____

Thanks to You, there are so many wonders to explore.
I won't hesitate to see and learn and discover.

AUGUST 18

Do you keep a journal? Why or why not?

20_ _ _____

_____

_____

_____

20_ _ _____

_____

_____

_____

20_ _ _____

_____

_____

_____

_____

Lord, help me to remember the ways
You reveal Your presence to me.

AUGUST 19

When your life feels like a tug-of-war, who
is on the other side of the rope?

20____ _____

_____

_____

_____

_____

20____ _____

_____

_____

_____

_____

20____ _____

_____

_____

_____

_____

*God, help me to know when to speak up
for what's right and when to quietly pray.*

Fruit of the Spirit question: How have you
been an example of patience?

20___ _____

_____

_____

_____

20___ _____

_____

_____

_____

20___ _____

_____

_____

_____

"Love is patient, love is kind. It does not envy, it does
not boast, it is not proud."—1 CORINTHIANS 13:4

You are speaking in front of 1000 people.
What will you talk about?

20___ _____

_____

_____

_____

20___ _____

_____

_____

_____

20___ _____

_____

_____

_____

_____

*I pray that my words will always be full of truth, faith, and
love, Jesus—whether I am talking to one person or a million.*

AUGUST 22

When has someone surprised you?

20___ _____

_____

_____

_____

20___ _____

_____

_____

_____

20___ _____

_____

_____

_____

_____

*God, help me to see the amazing things in other
people and in my surroundings.*

AUGUST 23

What would you like to add to your life?

20___ _____

_____

_____

20___ _____

_____

_____

20___ _____

_____

_____

_____

Lord, every good thing comes from You. Thank You.

What is the last thing you created?

20_ _ _____

_____

_____

_____

20_ _ _____

_____

_____

_____

20_ _ _____

_____

_____

_____

_____

"When God created mankind, he made them
in the likeness of God."—GENESIS 5:1

How do you feel about the dark?

20___ _____

_____

_____

_____

20___ _____

_____

_____

_____

20___ _____

_____

_____

_____

_____

Lord, sometimes I get anxious in the middle of the night. But when I remember that You are with me, I feel better.

When you move into your own home someday,
what would you like it to look like?

20___ _____

_____

_____

_____

20___ _____

_____

_____

_____

20___ _____

_____

_____

_____

"As you enter the home, give it your greeting. If the home is
deserving, let your peace rest on it." —MATTHEW 10:12-13

Who is a hero in your life?

20___ _____

_____

_____

_____

20___ _____

_____

_____

_____

20___ _____

_____

_____

_____

_____

God, thank You for the heroes in my life—the friends, family,
teachers, and neighbors who show they care about me.

What name would you go by if you were a rapper?

20___ _____

_____

_____

_____

20___ _____

_____

_____

_____

20___ _____

_____

_____

_____

_____

"Our mouths were filled with laughter, our tongues
with songs of joy." —PSALM 126:2

AUGUST 29

When have you felt a lot of pressure?

20___ _____

_____

_____

_____

20___ _____

_____

_____

_____

20___ _____

_____

_____

_____

_____

Jesus, help me to give my problems and stresses to
You. Thank You for helping me in every situation.

AUGUST 30

What is your favorite sport?

20___ _____
_____
_____
_____

20___ _____
_____
_____
_____

20___ _____
_____
_____
_____

Whether I sprint, volley, throw, or spin, I like to test the
physical and mental strength You give to me, God.

What does nature reveal to you about God?

20___ _____

_____

_____

_____

20___ _____

_____

_____

_____

20___ _____

_____

_____

_____

"Since the creation of the world God's invisible qualities—his
eternal power and divine nature—have been clearly seen, being
understood from what has been made."—ROMANS 1:20

What makes you really happy?

20___ _____

_____

_____

_____

20___ _____

_____

_____

_____

20___ _____

_____

_____

_____

*Thank You for making me smile, God. When I share silly
jokes with my friends or fun stories with my family, I
know that You are laughing right along with us.*

What do you look forward to in the new school year?

20___ _____

_____

_____

_____

20___ _____

_____

_____

_____

20___ _____

_____

_____

_____

_____

"Let us discern for ourselves what is right; let us
learn together what is good."—JOB 34:4

SEPTEMBER 3

What would you offer today for show-and-tell?

20___ _____

_____

_____

_____

20___ _____

_____

_____

_____

20___ _____

_____

_____

_____

Lord, I want to show and tell everyone about my faith and trust in You.

When have you worked really hard to make
something or earn something?

20___ _____

_____

_____

_____

20___ _____

_____

_____

_____

20___ _____

_____

_____

_____

_____

*Thank You for challenging me to push through obstacles,
God. It feels good to accomplish a task with You.*

SEPTEMBER 5

What are the most important words you heard this week?

20___ _____

_____

_____

_____

20___ _____

_____

_____

_____

20___ _____

_____

_____

_____

"There is no one like you, LORD, and there is no God but you, as
we have heard with our own ears."—1 CHRONICLES 17:20

SEPTEMBER 6

Do you like puzzles or dislike them? How about riddles?

20___ _____

_____

_____

_____

20___ _____

_____

_____

_____

20___ _____

_____

_____

_____

*You are the God of mysteries. Whenever something is too
amazing for me to understand, Lord, I will trust You.*

Who in your family has the strongest personality?

20___ _____

_____

_____

_____

_____

20___ _____

_____

_____

_____

_____

20___ _____

_____

_____

_____

_____

Families certainly are interesting! God, help the people in my
family encourage one another and give each other lots of grace.

What is your favorite dessert?

20___ _____

_____

_____

_____

_____

20___ _____

_____

_____

_____

_____

20___ _____

_____

_____

_____

_____

God, I want to thank You for every bite of good
food and every moment of a good day.

SEPTEMBER 9

Fruit of the Spirit question: How do you
show kindness and goodness?

20_ _ _____

_____

_____

_____

20_ _ _____

_____

_____

_____

20_ _ _____

_____

_____

_____

_____

*Jesus, I know I am being a good friend when I treat others the way You
do. Help me to look out for their well-being, speak the truth, and be kind.*

SEPTEMBER 10

When have you felt smart and empowered?

20___ _____

_____

_____

_____

20___ _____

_____

_____

_____

20___ _____

_____

_____

_____

"Do not throw away your confidence; it will be richly rewarded. You
need to persevere so that when you have done the will of God,
you will receive what he has promised." —HEBREWS 10:35-36

If you could turn a room in your house into your
own bedroom, which room would you choose?

20__ _____

_____

_____

_____

20__ _____

_____

_____

20__ _____

_____

_____

_____

Talking with You, God, is like being in our own special
place where we can share secrets with each other.

SEPTEMBER 12

What is the best gift you've ever received?

20___

_____

_____

_____

_____

20___

_____

_____

_____

_____

20___

_____

_____

_____

_____

God, every night at bedtime, I want to count the blessings
You gave me that day and say thank You.

SEPTEMBER 13

When did you last do a chore or something
helpful without being asked?

20___

20___

20___

"You will eat the fruit of your labor; blessings and
prosperity will be yours." —PSALM 128:2

Whom have you apologized to recently?

20___ _____

20___ _____

20___ _____

*God, saying I'm sorry is sometimes hard. Please help me
to do it when I know it's the right thing to do.*

SEPTEMBER 15

Would most people consider you messy or neat?

20___ _____

_____

_____

_____

20___ _____

_____

_____

_____

20___ _____

_____

_____

_____

_____

*Jesus, sometimes my room is a mess. Sometimes my emotions
are a mess. Will You help me to restore order?*

SEPTEMBER 16

When have you been proud of yourself?

20___ _____

_____

_____

_____

20___ _____

_____

_____

_____

20___ _____

_____

_____

_____

*I hope I make You proud, God. I want to live out
the dreams You have planned for me.*

If you had to share the message of the Bible without
using words, how would you do that?

20___ _____

_____

_____

_____

_____

20___ _____

_____

_____

_____

20___ _____

_____

_____

_____

_____

Lord, this week I will put my faith into action
so Your Word is evident in my life.

SEPTEMBER 18

Whom would you like to trade places with?

20_ _ _____

_____

_____

_____

_____

20_ _ _____

_____

_____

_____

_____

20_ _ _____

_____

_____

_____

_____

_____

God, help me pay attention to how other people are feeling and why.

SEPTEMBER 19

What do you have too much of?

20___ _____

_____

_____

_____

_____

20___ _____

_____

_____

_____

20___ _____

_____

_____

_____

_____

*Jesus, remind me to give to others when I can. I want my
first response to be to give in every situation.*

How does your family show love?

20___ _____

_____

_____

_____

20___ _____

_____

_____

_____

20___ _____

_____

_____

_____

_____

"Be devoted to one another in love. Honor one
another above yourselves."—ROMANS 12:10

SEPTEMBER 21

What have you found?

20___ _____

_____

_____

_____

20___ _____

_____

_____

_____

20___ _____

_____

_____

_____

Lord, I enjoy discovering new things in the world and in my life.

SEPTEMBER 22

What is your favorite fall activity?

20___ _____

_____

_____

_____

20___ _____

_____

_____

_____

20___ _____

_____

_____

_____

_____

You are the God of orange, red, and yellow leaves and the changing seasons. Thank You for always renewing Your creation.

Who or what cheers you up when you are discouraged?

20___ _____

_____

_____

_____

20___ _____

_____

_____

_____

20___ _____

_____

_____

_____

_____

Jesus, I need the kind of friend who will stick around even when I have hard days. Show me who in my life is that kind of faithful friend.

SEPTEMBER 29

What do you want to finish?

20_____ _____

_____

_____

_____

20_____ _____

_____

_____

_____

20_____ _____

_____

_____

_____

"My only aim is to finish the race and complete the task
the Lord Jesus has given me—the task of testifying
to the good news of God's grace."—ACTS 20:24

When have you felt separate from your family?

20__ _____

_____

_____

_____

20__ _____

_____

_____

_____

20__ _____

_____

_____

_____

God, help me to make the most of the special bond I have with my family.

What do you like to wear to dress up?

20___ _____

_____

_____

_____

20___ _____

_____

_____

_____

20___ _____

_____

_____

_____

_____

Lord, whether I am dressed up or I am dressed down, You think I am special.

SEPTEMBER 27

If you were to learn another language,
which one would you choose?

20__ _____

_____

_____

_____

_____

20__ _____

_____

_____

_____

_____

20__ _____

_____

_____

_____

_____

"If I speak in the tongues of men or of angels, but do not have love, I am
only a resounding gong or a clanging cymbal."—1 CORINTHIANS 13:1

SEPTEMBER 28

Do you prefer being in the country, in the city, or at the beach?

20___ _____

_____

_____

_____

20___ _____

_____

_____

_____

20___ _____

_____

_____

_____

*Jesus, wherever I go, You are there. No wonder I
like to visit so many different places!*

How has your view of God changed this year?

20___ _____

_____

_____

_____

_____

20___ _____

_____

_____

_____

_____

20___ _____

_____

_____

_____

_____

"Let the morning bring me word of your unfailing love, for
I have put my trust in you. Show me the way I should
go, for to you I entrust my life."—PSALM 143:8

What is the best gift you've ever given?

20___ _____

_____

_____

_____

20___ _____

_____

_____

_____

20___ _____

_____

_____

_____

*Jesus, teach me how to reach out to others with generosity
and serve them in a way that meets their needs.*

OCTOBER 1

If you were to help make a movie, would you rather
be the actor, director, writer, or cameraperson?

20___ _____
_____
_____
_____
_____

20___ _____
_____
_____
_____
_____

20___ _____
_____
_____
_____
_____

I am excited to discover more about my role in life. How can I best use
the gifts You have blessed me with, Lord? Please guide my steps.

When have you felt as if you didn't belong?

20___ _____

_____

_____

_____

_____

20___ _____

_____

_____

_____

_____

20___ _____

_____

_____

_____

_____

_Jesus, draw me close to You when I feel alone or separate from
the people around me. You are my security and safety._

OCTOBER 3

What is great about life right now?

20___ _____
_____
_____
_____

20___ _____
_____
_____
_____

20___ _____
_____
_____
_____

"Surely your goodness and love will follow me all the days of my life,
and I will dwell in the house of the LORD forever."—Psalm 23:6

OCTOBER 9

Whom do you want to visit?

20_ _ _____

_____

_____

_____

20_ _ _____

_____

_____

_____

20_ _ _____

_____

_____

_____

Who needs me today, Lord? Whom should I make the
effort to spend time with? Please help me to know.

OCTOBER 5

What is your favorite game?

20_____ _____

_____

_____

_____

20_____ _____

_____

_____

_____

20_____ _____

_____

_____

_____

_____

*Jesus, thank You for being my heavenly Father. You
enjoy hearing my laughter and seeing my joy.*

What does your family need to work on?

20___ _____

_____

_____

_____

20___ _____

_____

_____

_____

20___ _____

_____

_____

_____

_____

"Parents tell their children about your faithfulness."—ISAIAH 38:19

What is your biggest weakness?

20___

20___

20___

*Whenever I'm weak, that's an opportunity to trust Your strength,
Lord. Thank You for loving me when I succeed and when I fail.*

OCTOBER 8

Bonus: What question do you want to answer today?

20_____ _____

_____

_____

_____

_____

20_____ _____

_____

_____

_____

_____

20_____ _____

_____

_____

_____

_____

"Jesus replied, 'I will also ask you one question. If you answer me, I will
tell you by what authority I am doing these things.'"—MATTHEW 21:24

OCTOBER 9

If you found $100 on the bus, what would you do?

20__ _____

_____

_____

_____

_____

20__ _____

_____

_____

_____

20__ _____

_____

_____

_____

_____

Lord, I'm not sure what to do in some situations. Help me to act according to Your wishes and team up with You no matter what I face.

OCTOBER 10

What seems unfair?

20____ _____

_____

_____

_____

_____

20____ _____

_____

_____

_____

_____

20____ _____

_____

_____

_____

_____

*Lord, where there is injustice, help me to speak up. I want
to tell others about Your love and Your priorities.*

Do you focus more on things that have happened
or things that have not yet happened?

20___ _____

_____

_____

_____

_____

20___ _____

_____

_____

_____

_____

20___ _____

_____

_____

_____

_____

"Anxiety weighs down the heart, but a kind
word cheers it up."—PROVERBS 12:25

What is the best joke you've heard lately?

20___ _____
_____
_____
_____

20___ _____
_____
_____
_____

20___ _____
_____
_____
_____
_____

"A cheerful heart is good medicine." —PROVERBS 17:22

OCTOBER 13

What have you outgrown?

20__ _____

_____

_____

_____

20__ _____

_____

_____

20__ _____

_____

_____

_____

_____

*I will never outgrow Your wisdom and advice, God. At
every age, I can come to You for guidance and hope.*

Whom did you pray for most recently and why?

20__ _____
_____
_____
_____

20__ _____
_____
_____
_____

20__ _____
_____
_____
_____

"I tell you, love your enemies and pray for those who persecute you, that you may be children of your Father in heaven." —MATTHEW 5:44-45

OCTOBER 15

What is your earliest memory?

20___ _____

_____

_____

_____

20___ _____

_____

_____

_____

20___ _____

_____

_____

_____

When I face a difficult time, I can recall moments when You made everything okay, Lord. These memories encourage me.

OCTOBER 16

What does prayer feel like?

20__ _____

_____

_____

_____

20__ _____

_____

_____

_____

20__ _____

_____

_____

_____

_____

"The LORD is near to all who call on him, to all who
call on him in truth."—PSALM 145:18

Do you prefer to lead or follow?

20___ _____

_____

_____

_____

_____

20___ _____

_____

_____

_____

_____

20___ _____

_____

_____

_____

_____

_____

Show me when and how to lead, Jesus. And then show me when and how to be a devoted follower. Your big plans for my life will require me to do both!

Which do you like better, mornings or evenings?

20___ ___

20___ ___

20___ ___

*Jesus, I will think of You when I wake up and when I am about
to go to sleep. This will be how I measure a really good day.*

When do you feel distant from God?

20___ _____

_____

_____

_____

20___ _____

_____

_____

_____

20___ _____

_____

_____

_____

_____

"Come near to God and he will come near to you."—JAMES 4:8

If I had a spaceship, I would be headed for...

20__ _____

_____

_____

_____

20__ _____

_____

_____

_____

20__ _____

_____

_____

_____

_____

God, may I please have many adventures? I want to experience surprises and explore new places. Take me on a great journey!

What makes you sad?

20___ _____

_____

_____

_____

20___ _____

_____

_____

_____

20___ _____

_____

_____

_____

_____

Lord, when You see me cry and know that my heart is broken, You hug me. Thank You for helping me to feel Your embrace.

Fruit of the Spirit question: Why is faithfulness important?

20___ _____

_____

_____

_____

20___ _____

_____

_____

_____

20___ _____

_____

_____

_____

"Know therefore that the LORD your God is God; he is the faithful
God, keeping his covenant of love to a thousand generations of those
who love him and keep his commandments."—DEUTERONOMY 7:9

Where do you feel the most comfortable?

20___ _____

_____

_____

_____

20___ _____

_____

_____

_____

20___ _____

_____

_____

_____

Jesus, I don't always feel like myself with some people and in some places.
Please help me to be as comfortable with others as I am with You.

When did you have the most fun with your family?

20__ _____
_____
_____
_____

20__ _____
_____
_____
_____

20__ _____
_____
_____
_____

Dear God, I don't need big vacations or fancy games to enjoy my family. I like just being with them and talking about our day. Thank You for those simple times of connection.

OCTOBER 25

Who encourages or mentors you?

20__ _____

_____

_____

_____

20__ _____

_____

_____

20__ _____

_____

_____

_____

God, I want to have a godly mentor in my life. Please
help me know whom that should be.

If you could live anywhere in the world, where would you live?

20___ _____

_____

_____

_____

_____

20___ _____

_____

_____

_____

_____

20___ _____

_____

_____

_____

_____

*Lord, help me to care about people in other parts of the world. Teach
me how to pray for the needs of Your children everywhere.*

Baths or showers?

20___

20___

20___

Thank You, Lord, for washing me clean inside and out. Thank You for the rain, which renews Your creation.

OCTOBER 28

When have you broken a promise?

20__ _____

_____

_____

_____

20__ _____

_____

_____

_____

20__ _____

_____

_____

_____

_____

"Whatever your lips utter you must be sure to do, because
you made your vow freely to the LORD your God with
your own mouth."—DEUTERONOMY 23:23

OCTOBER 29

What decision do you have to make?

20____

20____

20____

*God, please help me to make smart choices. Thank
You for teaching me what is right.*

OCTOBER 30

If you could have only one view for a year,
what would you want to look at?

20___ _____

_____

_____

_____

_____

20___ _____

_____

_____

_____

_____

20___ _____

_____

_____

_____

_____

*When I pay attention, I notice so many new details around me. The colorful
leaves, the playful squirrels, the puffy clouds...I love to see Your works of art!*

What is your favorite color?

20___ _____

_____

_____

_____

20___ _____

_____

_____

_____

20___ _____

_____

_____

_____

*Thank You, God, for the world of Your colors—the aqua
ocean, yellow butter, purple plums, and pink sunsets.*

What is your prayer for the world?

20__ _____

_____

_____

_____

_____

20__ _____

_____

_____

_____

_____

20__ _____

_____

_____

_____

_____

"Pray in the Spirit on all occasions with all kinds of prayers
and requests. With this in mind, be alert and always keep
on praying for all the Lord's people."—EPHESIANS 6:18

Who is the craziest person you know?

20___ _____

_____

_____

_____

20___ _____

_____

_____

_____

20___ _____

_____

_____

_____

_____

God, give me wisdom when silly, wild, or interesting people challenge me to step beyond my comfort zone. I want to stretch and grow but never stray from Your truth.

NOVEMBER 3

What would you like your family to spend
more time doing together?

20___ _____

_____

_____

_____

20___ _____

_____

_____

_____

20___ _____

_____

_____

_____

_____

God, bless my family. When we get distracted, help
us keep our focus on You and on one another.

NOVEMBER 4

What makes you nervous?

20___ _____

_____

_____

_____

20___ _____

_____

_____

_____

20___ _____

_____

_____

_____

_____

"Do not be anxious about anything, but in every
situation, by prayer and petition, with thanksgiving,
present your requests to God."—PHILIPPIANS 4:6

If you could paint a huge image on the side
of a building, what would you paint?

20___ ___

_____

_____

_____

20___ ___

_____

_____

_____

20___ ___

_____

_____

_____

_____

God, what was it like to have all of the universe to fill with wonders from
Your imagination? Thank You for including me in Your incredible creation.

NOVEMBER 6

If you could be a person mentioned in
the Bible, whom would you be?

20___ _____

_____

_____

_____

20___ _____

_____

_____

_____

20___ _____

_____

_____

_____

*God, am I brave like Noah? Wise like Deborah? Trusting like Moses? Clever
like Esther? I pray to be all these things as my own story of faith unfolds.*

Do you need to forgive someone who is
difficult to forgive? Whom?

20___ _____

_____

_____

_____

20___ _____

_____

_____

_____

20___ _____

_____

_____

_____

Jesus, I choose to let go of my anger and forgive this person.
It's my turn to let Your grace flow through me.

When have you told a lie?

20__ _____

_____

_____

_____

_____

20__ _____

_____

_____

_____

_____

20__ _____

_____

_____

_____

_____

"Do not let any unwholesome talk come out of your mouths, but only what is helpful for building others up according to their needs, that it may benefit those who listen." —EPHESIANS 4:29

Do you feel like people know the real you?

20___ _____

_____

_____

_____

20___ _____

_____

_____

_____

20___ _____

_____

_____

_____

_____

*God, give me the strength and courage to be myself
and to allow my friends to be themselves.*

What do you want to create?

20___ _____

_____

_____

_____

20___ _____

_____

_____

_____

20___ _____

_____

_____

_____

_____

Every day is a chance to create something good and worthwhile.
Lord, stir my creativity and show me how to use it to glorify You.

NOVEMBER 11

If you wrote an inspirational song, what would it be called?

20___ _____

_____

_____

_____

20___ _____

_____

_____

_____

20___ _____

_____

_____

_____

"The LORD is my strength and song." —EXODUS 15:2 NLT

NOVEMBER 12

How are you a helper to your parents?

20___

20___

20___

*Jesus, show me how to support my parents in
new ways—even before they ask.*

NOVEMBER 13

What is your favorite candy?

20___ _____

_____

_____

_____

20___ _____

_____

_____

_____

20___ _____

_____

_____

_____

Tasting Your joy can be like tasting my favorite candy, Lord. You add a burst of happiness to a moment, a day, a lifetime.

Have you ever made another person feel bad?

20_____ _____

_____

_____

_____

20_____ _____

_____

_____

_____

20_____ _____

_____

_____

_____

_____

God, sometimes I say things without thinking about the damage my words could cause. Please help me to apologize when this happens.

If you started a company to help others, what would it do?

20___ _____

_____

_____

_____

_____

20___ _____

_____

_____

_____

_____

20___ _____

_____

_____

_____

_____

"Two are better than one, because they have a good
return for their labor."—ECCLESIASTES 4:9

Fruit of the Spirit question: How have you
shown gentleness to others?

20___ _____

_____

_____

_____

_____

20___ _____

_____

_____

_____

_____

20___ _____

_____

_____

_____

_____

*Lord, You are a gentle and loving shepherd. Help me to demonstrate
this same care through my actions, words, and prayers.*

What is your own definition of faith?

20___ _____

_____

_____

_____

_____

20___ _____

_____

_____

_____

_____

20___ _____

_____

_____

_____

_____

"Faith is confidence in what we hope for and assurance
about what we do not see."—HEBREWS 11:1

NOVEMBER 18

Who are you?

20___

20___

20___

You know everything about me, Lord. Please give me
insight into my special character traits and gifts.

If you could join an exploration team, where would you like to go?

20____ _____

_____

_____

_____

_____

20____ _____

_____

_____

_____

_____

20____ _____

_____

_____

_____

_____

God, whether I get to go to the far reaches of space,
Antarctica, or a new state, You will be my guide because You
created all the places I can ever dream of visiting.

NOVEMBER 20

Are you a candle, sparkler, or a firework?

20___ _____

_____

_____

_____

20___ _____

_____

_____

_____

20___ _____

_____

_____

_____

_____

"Live as children of light (for the fruit of the light consists
in all goodness, righteousness and truth) and find
out what pleases the Lord."—EPHESIANS 5:8-10

NOVEMBER 21

Who is the kindest person you know?

20__ _____

_____

_____

_____

20__ _____

_____

_____

_____

20__ _____

_____

_____

_____

_____

*Jesus, thank You for the generous and thoughtful people who
teach me how to receive kindness and give it to others.*

NOVEMBER 22

God must have a sense of humor, because...

20___ _____

_____

_____

_____

_____

20___ _____

_____

_____

_____

20___ _____

_____

_____

_____

_____

"God has brought me laughter, and everyone who hears
about this will laugh with me."—GENESIS 21:6

NOVEMBER 23

God knew you even before you were born! What
else is amazing about your Creator?

20___ _____

_____

_____

_____

20___ _____

_____

_____

_____

20___ _____

_____

_____

_____

*You know me and You love me. Help me never to forget this, Lord. I
want to base my entire life on these amazing, transforming truths.*

NOVEMBER 29

When you get sad news, do you prefer to
be alone or with someone?

20_ _ _____

_____

_____

_____

_____

20_ _ _____

_____

_____

_____

_____

20_ _ _____

_____

_____

_____

_____

*When I receive hard news, I will seek Your shelter and
protection, God. You hug me close and assure me.*

NOVEMBER 25

What are you thankful for?

20___ _____

_____

_____

_____

_____

20___ _____

_____

_____

_____

_____

20___ _____

_____

_____

_____

_____

"Let them sacrifice thank offerings and tell of his
works with songs of joy." —PSALM 107:22

NOVEMBER 26

Whom do you argue with?

20___ _____
_____
_____
_____
_____

20___ _____
_____
_____
_____
_____

20___ _____
_____
_____
_____
_____

God, please bring peace and calm to my difficult
relationship, and help us to support each other.

Describe what dinnertime is like at your house.

20___ _____

_____

_____

_____

20___ _____

_____

_____

_____

20___ _____

_____

_____

_____

Jesus, bless the time my family spends together. I pray for heart-to-heart talks that will help us walk side by side throughout the year.

NOVEMBER 28

What verse do you want to memorize?

20__ _____

_____

_____

_____

20__ _____

_____

_____

_____

20__ _____

_____

_____

_____

*Lord, Your Word is my guide, my lamp, and my hope. Give
me a great hunger to learn it and live it.*

NOVEMBER 29

How have you been or could you be a hero to someone?

20__ _____

_____

_____

_____

20__ _____

_____

_____

_____

20__ _____

_____

_____

_____

"We have different gifts, according to the grace given to each of us. If your gift is prophesying, then prophesy in accordance with your faith; if it is serving, then serve."—ROMANS 12:6-7

NOVEMBER 30

How does God help you during the day?

20___ _____

_____

_____

_____

20___ _____

_____

_____

_____

20___ _____

_____

_____

_____

"Whether you turn to the right or to the left, your ears will hear a voice behind you, saying, 'This is the way; walk in it.'"—ISAIAH 30:21

DECEMBER 1

I can't wait until...

20__ _____

_____

_____

_____

20__ _____

_____

_____

_____

20__ _____

_____

_____

_____

I don't have to know the future to know that You have good things planned for me, Lord. I'm excited to find out what tomorrow will bring.

DECEMBER 2

Where would you like to go for a mission trip?

20__ _____
_____
_____
_____
_____

20__ _____
_____
_____
_____
_____

20__ _____
_____
_____
_____
_____

*God, please use me as an example of Your compassion in
my home, school, church, and neighborhood. I'm ready to
spread Your good news anywhere You lead me.*

Would you rather be the age you are now
forever or keep getting older?

20___ _____

_____

_____

_____

20___ _____

_____

_____

_____

20___ _____

_____

_____

_____

*I know that I am complete and "enough" because of Your grace and
love. I don't need to do, earn, or prove anything for You to love me.*

DECEMBER 9

What miracle would you like to witness in your lifetime?

20___ _____

_____

_____

_____

20___ _____

_____

_____

_____

20___ _____

_____

_____

_____

_____

"You are the God who performs miracles; you display
your power among the peoples."—PSALM 77:14

If you had to stay in bed for a week, what two books would you
read to pass the time? What two movies would you watch?

20___ _____

_____

_____

_____

20___ _____

_____

_____

_____

20___ _____

_____

_____

_____

_____

*God, when I pray, You fill my mind and heart with good
things. As I seek joy, help me to also build up my faith.*

DECEMBER 6

How do you relax?

20___

20___

20___

I have some worries to give to You, Lord. Thank you for giving me Your peace.

Who is the most courageous person you know?

20___ _____

_____

_____

_____

20___ _____

_____

_____

_____

20___ _____

_____

_____

_____

Please help me to be courageous, God. Show me how to
support and celebrate the brave people I know.

When have you felt confident?

20__ _____
_____
_____
_____
_____

20__ _____
_____
_____
_____
_____

20__ _____
_____
_____
_____
_____

"I always pray with joy because of your partnership in the gospel from the first day until now, being confident of this, that he who began a good work in you will carry it on to completion until the day of Christ Jesus."—PHILIPPIANS 1:4-6

DECEMBER 9

You are digging for gold, but you find
something even better. What is it?

20_ _ _____

_____

_____

_____

20_ _ _____

_____

_____

_____

20_ _ _____

_____

_____

_____

_____

*Jesus, please help me to dream big. With You, there
are no limits. You are the God of miracles.*

What vegetable would you be willing to
eat with every meal for a month?

20__ _____

_____

_____

_____

_____

20__ _____

_____

_____

_____

_____

20__ _____

_____

_____

_____

_____

"It is written: 'Man shall not live on bread alone, but on every
word that comes from the mouth of God.'"—MATTHEW 4:4

If you were given $1 million to spend any way
you wanted, what would you do with it?

20___ _____

_____

_____

_____

20___ _____

_____

_____

_____

20___ _____

_____

_____

_____

I want to share what I receive, Lord. Direct my heart toward people who need
a kind word, a friend, a chance to be heard, or maybe a simple surprise gift.

DECEMBER 12

What do you need a break from?

20___ _____

_____

_____

_____

20___ _____

_____

_____

_____

20___ _____

_____

_____

_____

_____

Jesus, sometimes I worry and get stressed. Today I need
Your peace and perspective. You will help me through.

What do you think heaven is like?

20____ _____

_____

_____

_____

20____ _____

_____

_____

_____

20____ _____

_____

_____

_____

"Our citizenship is in heaven. And we eagerly await a Savior
from there, the Lord Jesus Christ."—PHILIPPIANS 3:20

DECEMBER 19

What would you like your future career to be?

20___ _____

20___ _____

20___ _____

God, I love to dream about what I might do someday and who I will become. Show me how to use the gifts You have given me. I want my entire life to be in Your hands.

DECEMBER 15

What is your favorite winter activity?

20___ _____

20___ _____

20___ _____

Lord, this is a season for the world (and my heart) to get
quieter. I want to take time to sit still in Your presence
to talk to You and to hear Your words for me.

DECEMBER 16

How long can you hold your breath?

20___ _____

_____

_____

_____

20___ _____

_____

_____

20___ _____

_____

_____

_____

"The Spirit of God has made me; the breath of
the Almighty gives me life."—JOB 33:4

DECEMBER 17

Who in your family has changed
the most in the past year?

20___ _____

_____

_____

_____

20___ _____

_____

_____

_____

20___ _____

_____

_____

_____

*God, You have the power to renew and transform us. I pray that
my family and I will grow daily to become more like You.*

DECEMBER 18

If you could be known for one thing, what would you want that to be?

20__ __

20__ __

20__ __

"He has shown you, O mortal, what is good. And what does the LORD require of you? To act justly and to love mercy and to walk humbly with your God."—MICAH 6:8

DECEMBER 19

Whom do you admire?

20___

20___

20___

*God, I admire some people for their talents and abilities. Others
I respect because they face tough times with faith. Help me to
learn from all the positive influences You have given me.*

DECEMBER 20

Fruit of the Spirit question: How and when
have you needed self-control?

20____ _____

_____

_____

_____

_____

20____ _____

_____

_____

_____

20____ _____

_____

_____

_____

_____

*Lord, I often need patience and self-control. When I'm struggling,
I will pray to You and rely on Your strength, not my own.*

How are you a good friend?

20___ _____

_____

_____

_____

_____

20___ _____

_____

_____

_____

_____

20___ _____

_____

_____

_____

_____

Jesus, You are the ultimate friend. Show me how to be a good listener
and encourager to my friends and the new people You put in my life.

DECEMBER 22

Whom do you like to tell first when you get good news?

20___ _____

_____

_____

_____

20___ _____

_____

_____

_____

20___ _____

_____

_____

_____

_____

"The angel said to them, 'Do not be afraid. I bring you good news
that will cause great joy for all the people.'"—LUKE 2:10

DECEMBER 23

If you were one of the Magi and were asked to bring a gift to baby Jesus, what would you bring from your life now?

20___ _____

_____

_____

_____

20___ _____

_____

_____

_____

20___ _____

_____

_____

_____

_____

Everything I have, own, or will ever possess belongs to You.
As a gift to You, I will tell others about Your love.

DECEMBER 29

Draw something that represents Christmas to you.

20___ _____

_____

_____

_____

_____

20___ _____

_____

_____

_____

20___ _____

_____

_____

_____

_____

Jesus, You were born so that everyone can know You
and trust the gift of Emanuel, "God with us."

DECEMBER 25

What do you love most about Christmas?

20___

_____

_____

_____

_____

20___

_____

_____

_____

20___

_____

_____

_____

_____

Happy birthday, Jesus. You were a baby who cried and
laughed and took first steps. Thank You for humbling Yourself
to show me and my family what love looks like.

DECEMBER 26

What do you wish someone had told you a year ago?

20__ _____

_____

_____

_____

20__ _____

_____

_____

_____

20__ _____

_____

_____

_____

_____

Lord, sometimes I have to learn about faith, hope, and trust by experiencing problems or mistakes. Growing up isn't easy, but You are always with me. Thank You, Lord.

DECEMBER 27

What question do you have for God?

20____ _____

_____

_____

_____

_____

20____ _____

_____

_____

_____

_____

20____ _____

_____

_____

_____

_____

_____

*I'm so relieved that I can bring anything to You. You won't consider my
questions too small or too difficult. You are my safe place, Lord.*

DECEMBER 28

What is your favorite inspirational song?

20___ _____

_____

_____

_____

_____

20___ _____

_____

_____

_____

_____

20___ _____

_____

_____

_____

_____

"Sing to the LORD, for he has done glorious things; let
this be known to all the world."—ISAIAH 12:5

DECEMBER 29

Whom do you want to tell about Jesus?

20___ _____
_____
_____
_____

20___ _____
_____
_____
_____

20___ _____
_____
_____
_____
_____

"I will tell of the kindnesses of the LORD, the deeds for which he is to be praised, according to all the LORD has done for us—yes, the many good things he has done for Israel, according to his compassion and many kindnesses."—ISAIAH 63:7

DECEMBER 30

What is the biggest change you've experienced this year?

20___ _____

_____

_____

_____

_____

20___ _____

_____

_____

_____

20___ _____

_____

_____

_____

_____

As I grow, Lord, life changes and so do I. Please help me adjust to new things.
I trust that the hard times and the good times will all lead me back to You.

DECEMBER 31

What is your wish for the new year?

20___ _____

_____

_____

_____

_____

20___ _____

_____

_____

_____

_____

20___ _____

_____

_____

_____

_____

"This is my prayer: that your love may abound more and more in knowledge and depth of insight, so that you may be able to discern what is best and may be pure and blameless for the day of Christ."—PHILIPPIANS 1:9-10

Unless otherwise indicated, all Scripture quotations are taken from the Holy Bible, New International Version®, NIV®. Copyright © 1973, 1978, 1984, 2011 by Biblica, Inc.® Used by permission. All rights reserved worldwide.

Verses marked NLT are taken from the *Holy Bible*, New Living Translation, copyright © 1996, 2004, 2007, 2013 by Tyndale House Foundation. Used by permission of Tyndale House Publishers, Inc., Carol Stream, Illinois 60188. All rights reserved.

Verses marked NASB are taken from the New American Standard Bible®, © 1960, 1962, 1963, 1968, 1971, 1972, 1973, 1975, 1977, 1995 by The Lockman Foundation. Used by permission. (www.Lockman.org)

Cover design, hand-lettering and illustration by Kristi Smith, Juicebox Designs

Interior design by Janelle Coury

Question of the Day
Copyright © 2018 by Harvest House Publishers
Published by Harvest House Publishers
Eugene, Oregon 97408
www.harvesthousepublishers.com

ISBN 978-0-7369-7418-9 (pbk.)

All rights reserved. No part of this publication may be reproduced, stored in a retrieval system, or transmitted in any form or by any means—electronic, mechanical, digital, photocopy, recording, or any other—except for brief quotations in printed reviews, without the prior permission of the publisher.

Printed in China

18 19 20 21 22 23 24 25 26 / RDS-JC / 10 9 8 7 6 5 4 3

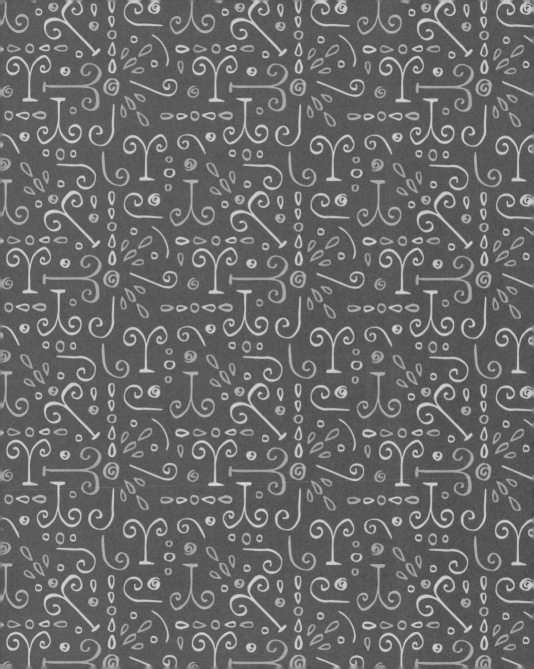

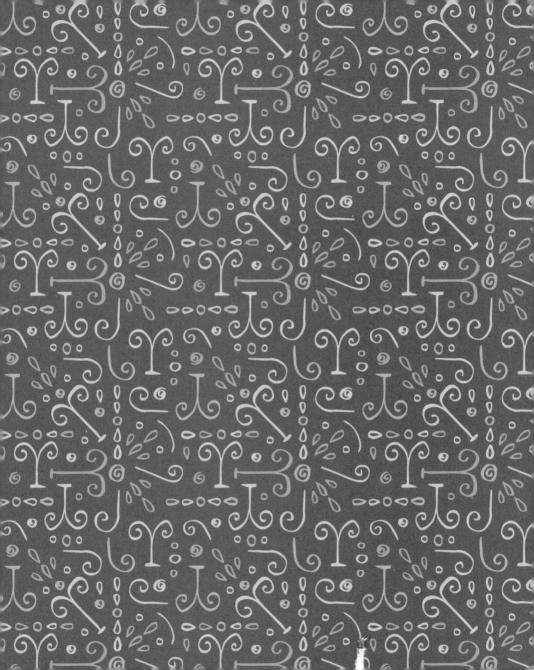